AF613994

a relatively small glimpse

poetic license Vol. 1

by dusty hamilton

Printed in the United States of America
First Printing, 2012
ISBN 978-1-105-60830-8

for me

CONTENTS

"It's been suggested that since I could probably make enough by writing half the year, why don't I relax the other half. I said, 'I would, but just to pass the time do you mind if i write?'"

--Isaac Asimov
1985 Nightwatch Interview on KCBS

salesman

opportunity knocked on my screen door
today
it was a salesman with an offer
(something i never tried)
youll be forever fit, feel like a rose
drawing in its scent
my moneypurse at the ready
i held it tight against me
and closed the inner door

opportunity knocked on my screen door.
and i didn't let him in

computers are a fad

do you really think that's all that she wrote
that they have the answer, that we should all gloat

the cream of the crop is yesterday's news
there's a race going on and you might just lose

download that new update or buy that i phone
they know you must have it, like a dog to a bone

it's going through trials they'll work out the bugs
you have to expect that, you say with a shrug

it's been outsourced for years and made in taiwan
but it's too late now, you're their little pawn

a house of cards is on which we stand
how long will it be 'fore we all need a hand

you're sure it won't break, you have faith in this scheme
what will it take to break out of this dream

and you have those passwords to keep it locked tight
do you sleep at night thinking everything's right

that hacker, that spammer never nods off a bit
he'll take all your money and make you submit

it's certain to freeze, destined to fail
just as you're one click away from checking your mail

it may not be pretty when it all goes to sh**
in the darkness is where you will soon sit

you play in a minefield of viral infection
your ipad has quite the bacterial collection

you'll be two seconds shy of sending your quote
and wishing you could find that antidote

cause when all of a sudden it just doesn't work
i bet you'll fall apart and just go bezerk

if your computer ends up in a big silent crash
just put it carefully outside, there in the trash

L, I'm Erick

a painful mistake i have paid,
to submit my heart so unpaved,
it wasn't so prudent,
(it needed improvement),
but this was the choice i had made

Notes:
it was my 1st limerick above

it was a flash in the pan
i dont even understand
how i never had tried
and woefully shyed
something today said i can

it was the first of its kind
not somthing i had in mind
but limerick or not
i gave it a shot
'cause this is how i unwind

when you first sit down
you may not hear any sound
but sooner than later
you'll find you can cater
to any of those around

there once was a pitter patter
i said, "by jove, what's the matter?"
you sat with a start
and boy, are you smart!
"I think that it's you, mad hatter"

in spring

the sprinkler ticks by
carefully dividing drops
one by one on grass

once

i was the one once
mistaken for a passing fog
i was drifting by
and you thought timc flcw
i was sitting listening
when you thought you were alone
i was in your thoughts
the night you couldnt sleep
i never told you more
but there i was neverless
i never told you id leave you
and youve never been the same

solomente

no sé el camino
esta vez
el uno que elija
no es mía
y yo no puedo ir
por lo que me esperará
pero tengo la sensación
de que usted no volverá
... Solas.

i don't know the way
this time
the one that you chose
is not mine
and i cannot go
so i will wait
but i have a feeling
that you will not return
... Alone.

por Cruz

i will comc to know
the mountains where you have lived
and have not returned

Un regalo.

Estoy dándome
Tú abres mi corazón
Mas yo recibo

she was just there

hearing you draw close
i could almost see your face
most beautiful creature
shaped just like a vase
i knew we had others
that begged for our attention
but just right this moment
she was mine
she never said hello
i never said goodbye
though in my bed she slept
in my heart she lie
we were not interrupted
& the time held still
she opened up her eyes
and stroked me down my side
there opened up within me
a welcome breath of air
a boyish delight
you'd wish you were there
the night could never pass
that my feelings be untrue
i want to die like this
tonight i want to live

mt

scattered broken terrifying
looters have taken all my
memories and adjectives

all thats
left
is..

annexed

simple things
laughter
touch
wink

afterthoughts

your scent on my pillow
is all i have
today

sailing home

There a vast quiet.
Youll find a noticeable calm.
A luxurious way to sip your coffee.
Up on the deck alone.
The way a morning comes out.
Like it was meant to be.
Gentle tidal splashes licking the shore.
its me floating home
nothing but the silence
hear the cars if youre still.
easing into their beats
a soft background refrain
a crane stirs the solid waters plane
and you just realize
youre really here

the inside me

you might think im joking
and tooting my own horn
i will just begin
you were not the first
of the ladies plenty
i couldnt count the numbers
nor would you want me to compare
i am a cauldron of excess
quality impure
lucky i could think of it
or damn infatuation
ive been so had and noticed
but alone instead
that i cant enjoy them forever
i am not at a loss
i regret my slaving
over skin and technique
i may be good @ loving
but damaged here inside
ive had my share and yours
one for every year
the babes were gorgeous
and never did i cheat
they deserved the finest
i brought them some
but i swear to you
tried to make each peak
i loved it at the time
a fetish, orgasmic plan
doesnt seem so sinful now
to make them smile below
you may think me unclean
or as if they were the prey
i never thought it wasted
i never thought it planned
i just had an endless search
for the one that was forever
i think ive found her now
and my quest is over
ive waited nine whole years
to fall in love again
matured and growed up now
id die to lose her trust

i have a sure thing coming
a pleasurable delight perhaps
or a seat in coach
all the way to hell
so i wanted to thank you
all you from my past
who waited and came with me
to see if i could compete
i only am the one im now
wrought by your warm chisels
you kept my fire billowed
an inner-oven-heated clay
i leave my past wholeheartedly
starting now anew
i give up my whorish ways
and think of now today

self portrait

the artist has awoken
to his daily grind
a puzzle soon unbroken
runs within his mind
laid upon his sheets
of oil pastel and base
were measures tempos beats
enunciating grace
his vast wardrobe of scenes
the patterns and the tails
beautifully woven into genes
or sewn upon his sails
while the public peruses
a feeling starts unbroken
it really quite confuses
but thoughts are soon provoken
for what he had laid
the sculptures he had pined
he would not be paid
nor contract ever signed
on the objects that he chooses
he must have some perspective
whether it angers or amuses
he must remain subjective
his favorite thing you'd find
near him just in case
always is a paper lined
& only briefly, empty space

su novio

i shuttered that night,
when i heard your words
"i love you but..."
i never heard the end
you might have seen it happen
i must have glowed i bet
not a blush, but a light within
i filled like a teacup
and overflowed its saucer
i never saw it coming
in my heart i ran
i danced and held my heart
delight could not describe
i never had imagined
a time i'd have, as this
i brought myself to now
back down from my cloud
shook my head and wondered
what else you had said
i knew it was suggestion
a focus on condition
of how i lived my life
the importance of decision
i had to want to change
to set and reach my goals
remember whats important
and find her there and then
i had belief she'd wait
patient. not unconscious
she had to break the silence
the elephant in the room
i've seen the late she spoke of
and held it in my glass
my ship and land apart
i had a fighting chance
i want to remember
the effortless flight i took
when she said those words
"i love you, but..."

H3

hurriedly it spins
clad in grip of gravity
but it slowly dies

practice no

know it
there is no it
i know it
no

H2

she is beautiful
in every way a flower
sincerely, the rain

uh uh uh..

“uh uh uh, "
she shakes her finger at me
in her little way
that melody i know so well.
i smile
a curving corner || bite
wonder/knows she's serious
she teases with her lips
i draw her close upon me
she locks me in her eyes
you know i want you badly
i want in -your thighs
she knows i will respond
that i will resist
but just for that moment
my heart beats treble in my head
blood courses thru body
adrenaline shot increased
if i cant have you now
you know i'll soon want more

H1

i am enchanted
by something you have today
something you have said

softly spoken verbs

its not a race
iface
writings just my
something i enjoy
if i dont touch a thought
and it flies out the window
will i be
alone?

what..?

i m that last bite
i m the sour cream
the one you always wanted
well enjoy away
why do you stay
is there someone youd eat instead
i ant believe that look
as if i give offense
the barrier
aint English - i spin balls with technique
nor body language either
but you look at me:
a backhanded, slapping glance
a pitch
a sound.
i recoil to in shame
whatever do i do or say
you never let me know
i sit apologizing
until in my arms you flow
whew that was a close one
to be edited
im off work
i called it quits
a poem a day
im a head of schedule
but in my head
grow dandelions
and i just cant resist
weeding out these flowers
and shoveling
manure
if you had my problems
youd press refresh at once
but if you knew the answers
why would you care to share
im on an outbound mail Truck
im headed out to greece
im on a delivery i'll be back
im sure
but if i could take a minute
and swim in the canals
the water so blue
it glistens

i really must be going
i hear the churchbell ring
it is not every day
i feel so cleansed as now
what is this world i live in
that lacks a tidy living
/evening
spent with my wife
she knows i passion
i relent to come to bed
unless to sit beside her
or make her eyes roll back
but if i could ;stay up n write
that id do instead
i really cant compete
with the visions on my paper
they need to be organized
in such and such a way
dont make me go right now mom
we just started this game
havent you been young once
havent you felt the same
you make a boy out of me
you make me a stud
i never thought or had
a dream
im in right now
so let me get my sleep, i mumbled
its mourning in a while

new

experimental pizza
coming down the pike
ive added all your suggestions
ive added all your suggestions
no topping does it lack
its like mixing all the colors
and ending up with black

le poéme

certainement je voudrais aller
mais, mes ailes ont été coupé
je sera séjour

the sentence

no sense in getting upset
it gives you no reward
will not help ;you with that paper
you cant bottle it ether
nor can u give it - a way
time will tell
if yore doing well
"honestly", was to blame

listen..
where once i felt so close
a deep cavity remains
when i go back and think
opportunity had passed me by
without a sound
like
"i'm sorry"

nontranslated word

Act 1

selfish.
that one word should stand alone
it brought us together
you(.) understood
(that eager was her void)
i beg you to respond
shh...
quiet..
..
shhh

. . she's calling out your name

Act 2

your response unwritten
scared
i taught you that word, selfish
you taught me survival
now whatyou gonna do with it
the secret to her power
if i might suggest
unlocking the door between

Act 3

ar u well
r u deep n thought
c ant u remember
what did she say
> enough for 1000 lives,
her fears are unimaginable
she is a person, dusty,
but new.
'i read her like a book
i took her as a shower'

i hear you're getting married

poetic license revoked,
clock out
hey, you start training the new guy tomorrow
maybe something will open up in another area.
i hear uh..Joe, down in birthday cards, is gonna retire next year, maybe
this,
well, this is hard for me too, okay?
it's a little late to get emotional now.
don't make me call security
look, just hand in your key on your way out tonight
don't even worry about tomorrow, either.
no, there's nothing to reconsider

because you just don't have that emotion anymore
i wish i could help out, we've tried everything;
we've been down that road before.
you don't have to get it, look, give me a beaten, crippled, old man .
HE's on the edge; HE could be talent
things are just going too well in your life for this company
and at this time we wish to sever our contract with you

we just don't have work for you anymore.
look, if someone close to you dies or...i don't know, you become an alcoholic
or
something, give us a call. other than that,
i'm sorry too. there just isn't any work for a "satisfied" poet.
Hey, i hope to hear from you soon, huh?
Oh and Arthur, break a leg!

i’ve got it! i lost it

pluck and prod and give it a nod
and stop all this selfish denial
get on the ball you're losing control you need to get some help
therapy help or drugs or relations what have you to say to that

this is my form of release
now leave me in peace or i'll call the police

your sentence structure
your conversational tone
i cannot imagine untrue

of
course

steady; thorough
post-act?

ex-act-ly

i am >

no velcro tie of lie

i never knew a passion so true, a life id never end
edit but never undo

i love . and That is enough.

nothing comes to mind

a book of poetry is never finished
it goes untouched, alone
it is no friend of mine

i do not like the rhyme
its near my bed instead

"wouldnt it be funny if instead money
we had only honey
our wallets would be quite a mess
these are things in my head i confess"

how can you read such pitiful banter
it doesnt touch you at all
its either mindless drivel
or cheerful endeavors
the meanings are always to
open and blue. no place for inner inspection
weve been inserted diverted postponed
the message is lost or undecidedly clear
there is nothing for me here
too deep is this canyon
its range underwater
i'm skiing and it's indoors
the prose hits my nose and up it goes
and i feel no magnetic attraction
the style keeps changing
the wording verbose
next

stop.

get out of my head.
was it something He said?
i can't forget that one though
i try
a valium, an upper for supper, you'll see
i'll forget all this nonsense real soon
but before i cant handle
any verse in this fashion

i must be remarkably board
or obnoxiously sloppilly drunk
for if you dont save me
or slap me i pray
i'll be prey - victim of his will i be
he got me again, thats it, im in
in his lost train of thought
a tunnel and its taking me down
and around
its never been this bad before
Doesnt he stop
isnt he through
is there a mechanical malfunction
i think hes morose and depraved and deprived
i think i'll start a line too.
perhaps i could write, i'll just take a bite
it can't possibly be that hard
now what comes to mind
is i have to unwind
and this may be just my thing
i set pen to paper
and stanza to verse
and google all my wording first
i'm in charge and i'm living large
i'm going to show you poetry

let this be a lesson
yep! this smith and wesson
will kick the sh** out of you

-write on

one poem, one

all life has meaning, all but one.
the most repetitive one of all:

ive got a notion a lotion a potion
not a portion.
abortion
ive got a train my brain; its plain its insane
it comes with remarkable dread instead
of the other which i cannot discuss
its too heavy for you to see me bear

its not indecision or digestion or cancer
its not impossibly define or divine
just a notion a push a wish a crush
a past and a future thats bright
impossibly crooked past on a river of glass theres a mast
and a lite and a match
to see through the fog or igniting the soul in a blizzard or blast

its not angina or the vagina thats made me feel unpleasant
ive never had finer.. i mean, this diner this pheasant its all been so pleasant
reason this season is thought and control and learning something so new
of myself and my worth and my undying thirst to find the one who loves you

i never seen anyone with that look in their eye when at me they
see me within

joyously boastful clad in glad is rad you'll see
if i get senti-mental or semi-rigid it's not from this flight of fancy
to have you within and a/part is smart but impossibly slow
id rather be in a story of us; a liquid with you as a brush
your laugh fills my heart and it shudders asleep
and i realize im holding my breath.
your smell it dwells it lingers. my fingers.
have burn marks you've touched me so deep. in sleep.
i weep and it creeps up my sole up my head away is my dread instead its
surreal
I feel.
It's real. i kneel and heal and stutter and stammer "four more!"
i whisper, "together," ("there is no other nor will ever there be")
i could never be better or sweater. for that matter sweeter.
its neater and nearer your heater

your heart beating rhythmically true. you're the glue
That, holds us together like no other. I say, "again."
you grin, "listen," "it's in." its the new thing to do
no one in charge, is taking over, i'm in. i am impossibly you.

is there a reason for my undying love
for this unstoppable smile?
it must be hope. its no longer the dope. because of you ive turned life around
its sound its flurry its word
undelivered undeposed unreposed
you've seen my best and i hint at the worst and you never flinch or give up.
how you dont throw up your hands i dont understand
this must be impossible you. a cape and an "s" is what you should wear
dressed in red white and blue. hands on your hips, a fine looking chick you'd
be

so with discression you teach me, your lessons
have pleasured my heart. pictures dont make, can't create
what (i) was i)(saying

what am i saying, that i yam what i yam
or you're my yo to my yo
i've just never been happier or in such delight some nights all right?
i just love you.

a level playing field doesn't make me handicapped

dont fix me.
im not a project. im not a ghetto im not asyntax
im not a sentence
im not a noun im not a thing i m not clay
im coming to realize all life has a pattern
of worry and healthy demise
its really quite beautiful if youd give it time. there are things about it that give me a shine
d d dont believe me now, (I'm) fine
but i'll feel the same tomorrow.

you've lost something

you don't look at me with that tear in your eye
when i leave anymore

maybe ive taught you to be tough
or is it brave

or maybe ;you dont care, are you getting used to this
pattern
of neglect

so impassionate
that your hugs feel like shrugs when they were like drugs

love.

Notes:
a poem to my daughter

10 Rules of Poetry

what poetry must do (he spat)
there are forms to follow (rats)
the most important thing
not passion or person
spice is nice and sure is a cure
but keep it rollin
if you please
reaction is not
condition
ed

box din

stepped out of my box and into the fire!
its not from youth or for my desire
its for the blood oath! its for the battle!
life is a sport and you have a saddle,
but when you look close, it's only a rattle

well allow me to retort

my online submittal is nothing to baulk
ive written them poetry, rhythm, or blurbs
most publishers have only sidewalk chalk
they sit in their studios; some smokin the herbs

i know i write some hard hitting stuff
and sometimes a piece on a snowball's fluff
and when i set pen to paper and start to see rhyme
i kick off my shoes and start to unwin(d)
it's not always cheerful and happy or rose
some's not even poetry its actually prose

i don't always go with the flow
though i might see a pattern
the geese follow roads too
but it's not to saturn

there's something in me that asks out loud
something shiny and tiny
and of it i'm proud
i feel punctuation's an option
capitalization a sin
unless you have a reason within.

there are rules to poetry, sir
the schematic stanza
and free verse is quant
but didn't you go to DeAnza?

yo, a-oh, lend me your ears
don't tell me that all of these years
in classrooms and workshops
have given you vision,
maybe you'd learn more
had you been to prison.
or had a life of decision
you've too much precision
inside that head
them's clouds outside
or haven't you read
there's emotions and feelings
and all of them sad
don't testify to me

i'm not so bad
no, not me, i'm a good little boy
i'd just get a kick of you being their toy.
i'm not saying i've had a life of color
i'm just here like you, a brother
and if i offend
let me just spend
a second to be like no other

I will learn your style.
Just give me a while,
"Rome wasn't built in a day."
Hey whats the worst?
I may never get off first?
Sit and enjoy, be gay.

i'm enjoying the ride
no limits, no pride.
no cheerful endeavor
to be clever
or stick with the same old game
think out of the box
and into the rhyme
(whoa, that's heavy)
so
look ol' man, i don't run with the herd
i ain't fresh from Berkeley
you birkenstock brass
so make like a tree
and kiss my

breath

breathing
heavy
hot
&sudden
last time
but now
for the first time
i awoke
and knew you were there
the rumpled comforter
no bedding could not hide your sleeping splender
i was home but in my house i was not
vacant we left
my door open, we had hurried from there
was it last night?

i could almost believe it was years ago
how awesome a feeling of waking every new day as i did today
pulled in a silent, driving force we had gone
close to avoid the night's desolate chill
but without a touch or word

as wife and husband we would do it so many times,
someday
i knew it so plainly beautifully true
but that night we had that closeness that i have never known
i see that moment as closely as now
outside, in that union
your blanketed youngest slept, carried in my arms
worn out from the day

we eloped to your space
an unspoken unseen look did pass between us
"care not to wake the children"
and we glanced (& counted) the one, two,..
three, there she is, angels who carefully lain their heads
snuggled in the warmth of home and happiness
together we pulled out the bed and with care
gave the 3 each of us space

not a kiss was needed between her and i..
we intuitively laid our tired bodies close
and were quick to fall asleep

and i smiled, this morning. while you all slept.

right –by me

we're not the innocent
we're not the blamed
we're not the victims
but we're not the chained

we get the sentence
we get the term
we get the hook
but we get the worm

we're not heroic
we're not complacent
we're not down heartened
but we're not impatient

we get the verdict
we get the time
we get the guilty
but we get the grime

we don't do it for money
we don't do it for blame
we don't do it for vengeance
but we don't do it for fame

we'll get a parade
we'll get a mention
we'll get a bullet
but we'll get a pension

we do it for children
we do it for dope
we do it for ladies
but we do it for hope

we got a handshake
we got a wave
we got a smile
but we got a grave

control

i fight against the breakers
the tide is under rated
i think im making progress but i cant stay put
i assume a course correction
and head out to sea
perhaps i'll float instead

160 or less

O u t. There.

why do i rhyme
why take the time
its a sport to me
a gamble to Be

play thru

sail
sail away from here
just keep running with the wind
my reach is wide
id go out in a big wave
past the discorporation
through the oil slick
toward that peace of quiet
sailing free
main sheet cleated
just bouncing thru these white caps
everlasting speed

ready,
now hard over and run
no one to stop me
no ship in my path
close my eyes and hold that course

a simple procedure
to leave that quay
to jet from the slip
to cast it all behind you
just heave that sail
theres nothing to worry
no cares in the world
no one to call wait
no path you can't take

so sail away

make ready,
plot a course
the oceans and bays
are open for sport

the destination is no issue
where you go doesnt matter
you might surge on ahead
with the wind at your back
but i tell you i like it
out there on the waves

i'll put down my anchor
and pull out my charts
and kick back in the open
with a satisfied grin
a cup of tea in my hand
and out of reach of land

there's no where you can't go
no place you can't tack
when you're out on the water
it's as simple as that

the silence is golden
the piece is unreal
you can't buy it or rent it
or see it online
just take a trip sailing
you'll go out of your mind

Es no bueno.

es no mi gusta
after i thought we got so far
she still cuts me like a knife
through the hoops and around the potholes
the cliffs and through the breakers
she still guts me with that shiv
so gentle she is and i never see it coming
she tore me below the ribs
i can piece myself together
going fine on all fours
i think shes changed her tune
if youd look at us tomorrow
none would ever see the damage
all is fine and good
a perfect twosum we'll be
you might not think it possible
to love someone so much
but it tears my heart in half
when she hurts me like she does
perhaps the next day or the next
if i explain it once again
i could stop these wounds
i could get respect.
but i foresee the same thing
a hook beneath that bait
but doesnt it look nice
and i feel so at ease
she gives me besos and makes me laugh
and it becomes all good

Eso es mi vida.

just show up

(by d.h)

room to improve

the

reasons to grow fancy silk tie

close

a place to begin hair parted neatly

shiney black shoes

& something to show freshly starched shirt

friends gather round

smiles and tears

thoughts

good wishes

respectable dress

silence

(is there no other way)

for her

and here i sit, sat fumbling, thinking
wondering among my thoughts, blinking
wherever will i be
when the time i know shall pass
my youngster so far and gone.
alone i'll be
so forgotten
so mis-placed
distance growing evermore
time passing aging maturing
ceaselessly i implore
my wishes ignored unspoken
driving me mad all the while
separation deviation
untouched unable unresponsive.
kept unnurtured by her touch
turning twisting time is wasting
draining life each day
not for me alone is my sorrow
but for her
unknowingly breaking
down without me
battered withered dwarfed
and orphaned
how do i let go on?
how one branch does not break
under increasing strain
i never want to know.
for pain has no reward,
please be kind, rewind

(is there no other way)

Notes:
undelivered but written to D---, my ex, at a time when i allowed my daughter to spend the summer away from me; to be with her mom in North Carolina, away from all she knows. I was so nervous I'd never get Haley back. D--- had agreed to let me keep her for the rest of the school year, from to about March to July 9th, and I had promised that D---'s graciousness would be met with my equal trusting attitude likewise during the summer. And then she'd return to me for the next school year here in California.
But at the end of the summer, D--- was having second thoughts, it broke my soul and i wrote this poem.

TODAY my daughter was returned to me!! It's August 18th and my Haley can spend the full school year here. I can sleep easy now. For so long I was hoping for this day.
And my trust in my ex and my good fortune have been rewarded.
I just wish this fear of losing my baby again could be erased.

haiku this

DAY TO RECHARGE
REBOOT
NAP

-clumbsy-

asseyez-vous and refrain
if you're quiet we'll remain

simple structure, boxed and wrapped
just your size and newly packed.

emblazoned and admired, tightened to the teeth
if i could just get my fingers, a little ways beneath

i've come to reach your heart, you took me in your fold
i cant believe the passion, and that i plan to hold

we didn't need a thing, had no want of money
the look a kiss a stare at you, you're mine forever honey

i'd run and tell my brother. i'd tell it to my son
such a delightful thing is love, when that you have undone

to touch the silver locking hasp. i fumbled it again
dont you see how much i want for you and i to sin

it's you that i am after, that's why in here we lay
"keep still" i say, "remember, it's not as if i'm gay"

i don't want to know the secret, i want it to be new
it only takes one woman but blushes me and you

be off! you bless-ed garment; im ready to explode
the fire restrained but kindled. cant stop to reload

you'd think there'd be instructions; i'd think there would be too
this thing's a mess and i confess, i never really knew

we're smiling at the present, we're gasping at delight
furious my fingers flew, when i caught that sight

alas they are so splendid. i'll bite my lip in two
oh my god how you just quivered, and that is when i blew

cast away

mooring loose
sallow
drifting
regret
canted
heeled
drowning
untethered
punctured
sinking
depth
caged
barren
blue
sinking

a look at sadness

i feel the need to grieve
i am so torn apart
i feel so alone

$\sum$ **(You?)**

how light my heart is felt
when it first awaked .

to an eternity
thought of you

begun to begin
your song
a silent concerto :

bermudic sand
or the intricate pebble road
assembled

,built,purposed
a gift a shower a spark
a lighted gas throughout

for perchance you might stay
a while
and gaze .

or sigh .or spit. or swallow

me?
i've reached you
a tiny cog has sprung

escape wheel or anchor
i'll never really know

you've filled my blanks
,crossed my t's
and lightened the load i've carried

you've set the compass new
and i don't want to leave .

<this time>

this shore
it's home :
grass green , water blue

glistening or clapping
or waving at the show?

that it's all for you
do you realize

share in my splendor
or can it in a jar ;

i'd gladly take my time again

to look .
Into your deep brown eyes
so
knowing asking smiling

the aches you hear are here,
don't you see
choices held
memories made or a bit of each

background noise or life begun
sprouted flourished winged

all part all pure all heart
my simple gift or nudge
, for you, you for my love

there is one cold hard fact
upon this factory floor :

that i am blessed for seeing .
the beauty
that watchis us.

<Dénouement>

<exit>

the good news is

i've bypassed a lot
and i've seen a few
arteries like this here
are nothing new

you're filling them up
and that's not a joke
you expect me
to give them a poke

i'll ream them and graft them
and give you a chance
if it werent for me here
you'd be food for the ants

you need to be careful
and watch what you eat
can't you start to feel
your blossoming seat

it wont be long now
you'll be seeing your maker
they'll sell all your goods
if there are any takers

at the table remember
its better to pass
cause gravy and grease
is too heavy a mass

i've done my work here
you're going to live
now from that pocketbook
you'll have to give

i do not come cheap
but you'll pay the price
your off on your own now
and isn't that nice.

it’s a sickness with me, don’t you see

theyll close the door and lock it and open in 30 days
i better bring my pencil, i'll be going at it in spades
dont give up now, the writings on the wall
dont make me leave till i copy it all
how can this be proper in such a space as this
i thought this was punishment, to see what i would miss
but i cant stop this car from crashing, im coming down the road
these thoughts in my head, ive got to empty this load

the dock

the dock swayed beneath my feet
glanced below and smiled
never to return
darkness reigns and i have wept
for you to understand
it all fell down around me,
it all has come apart.
these veins run deep within
and here i stand, battered
bruised
bruised
kneeling
beaten down
torn asunder
catastrophic loss
unable to go on
alone
breathless pain
pierced and bleeding
ill fed and unwell
tear
the hint of your name brings tears
forgotten
standing without you gives me chills
left
a lump in my heart is what i know
unneeded
suffering without understanding
how could i let myself need you so much
why are you so important
why cant i give up
am i living hell
so that i can repair
or being self mutilated
i am cast away
i'm discarded
carrion
driven by impulse
lacking my light in the storm
backtracking
flooded
winded
beaten

dead
how much suffering will suffice
how much pain are you worth
well let me ask myself
how long did i plan for my love to last
why cant i just stay down
why cant i stop this rain
why cant i stop this wind
"there a storm a comin" the old man said with a smile
and he pointed that bony finger upward and then leveled it at me
the light caught his eye and i knew there was no avoiding that curse
i wouldn't be forgiven i couldn't be so lucky
it would swell upon me like a great ocean upon my chest
i would heave and pant as it stomped upon me, face up on the sand
and it would smother me with every wave
a great wall would beat down on me
and death was not my friend
i am destined to feel
dormant

and He would shake his head and deliver
another punch and a kick
a lesson i just can't grasp
a feeling i just cant acquire
you'll know when your dead because you just wont care
and bloodied, drenched, and sobbing, i rose again
so that the wave could blast at me and i fell back
and dragged toward the sea in the black moonlight
fingers gashed raw against the rocky outcrops
not so peaceful today, is it
it turns evil at night, and its only just begun
no one is able to help; how ironic it all seems
that there is NO ONE at all who can help me from feeling this way
even She probably couldn't stop this train, im already off the tracks
and ive got quite a load behind me, no
im in it for the long haul.....

T-minus

in the time we have left

zero counter reset

this tme pay attention

listen

step up

theres nothing on tv
theres something in your head
its driving you insane
you havent gone to bed

you keep it bottled up
you wont tell a sole
but you better break soon
because youve lost control

i know it would be wiser
if you had seen it coming
we cant all have the same life
we cant all have that fire

they all tried to warn you
to tell you of the danger
you shook your head at them
but you started to perspire

even if you let go
you know it will not matter
be honest with yourself
stop being such a liar

we have all these ideas
of how good our lives can be
if only you had one chance
to be what you admire

Submission

here's my submission
for your admission
perfect in every detail
for syndication
my name in quotation
or you'll delete my e-mail

on certain pages
my brain has had wages
though seemingly simpleton verse
with a snort and a laugh
you'll cut it in half
placing the corpse in a hearse

are there any takers
you goddamn heartbreakers
to my reason or rhyme
what i am saying
is you won't be paying
it's just a big waste of time

so this i submit
if you will permit
before your omnipotent might
this heart and soul
is really quite droll
something that isn't quite right

though i may have slaved
it will not be saved
it's one you're sure to erase
it won't get attention
there'll be no ascension
not a shot in this database

there should be a directive
to see my perspective
but you'll say with a look in your eye
that you'll send your regards
(but those flowers have barbs)
publication of this poem must die

so if i refrain
from now showing you pain
this is a line you can quote
in my future memoirs
i will not have scars
nor will you be a footnote.

"...its all there, on paper, and I wont be gone, it'll be there."

--Isaac Asimov
1988 Interview with Bill Moyer

dh

(1973-   )

Born in Sacramento, California and raised in the San Francisco Bay Area, Dusty Hamilton has begun a poetic journey that he's ready to share. In his daily life, he is passionate about the relationships with his daughter and other true love -- it is this romance to a beautiful and mysterious woman from Apatzingán that spurred a renewal of his poetic license. He spends his free time sailing, writing, and on nature's path.

i feel punctuation's an option
capitalization a sin
unless you have a reason within.

www.ingramcontent.com/pod-product-compliance
Ingram Content Group UK Ltd.
Pitfield, Milton Keynes, MK11 3LW, UK
UKHW040558210726
13854UKWH00008B/1391